Stories of China

Chorus Singing from the People

by Wang Yang   Ju Zi

新世界出版社
NEW WORLD PRESS

First Edition 2009

By Wang Yang and Ju Zi
Translated by Shi Wei
Edited by Li Shujuan
Photo provided by Qin Zhaonong, Qin Fengjing, Hei Ke,
and the Love on the Grassland Chorus Group
Cover Design by Han Ying

ISBN 978-7-80228-998-7

Published by
NEW WORLD PRESS
24 Baiwanzhuang Street, Beijing 100037, China

Distributed by
NEW WORLD PRESS
24 Baiwanzhuang Street, Beijing 100037, China
Tel: 86-10-68995968
Fax: 86-10-68998705
Website: www.newworld-press.com
E-mail: frank@nwp.com.cn

Printed in the People's Republic of China

Contents

A year ago, correspondents from the Deutsche Welle (DW) reported on an interesting scene in the parks of Beijing. According to the report, a new collective activity has emerged gradually in recent years. On Sundays, many citizens gather in groups in various parks of Beijing to practice chorus singing. The groups were of different sizes, ranging from several people to several hundred and sometimes over one thousand. Initially, the people sang songs mostly from the former Soviet Union or the Chinese songs from the 1960s and 1970s. Despite the Chinese media's praises for the activity, the report raises doubts as to whether the participants take part in the choruses simply for fun or for other reasons altogether.

Public choruses are seen in Beijing as well as in other cities

▶ Chorus singing by middle-aged and senior citizens can be seen in the parks of big and medium-sized cities all over China.

than one thousand people stood around a pavilion singing, conducted by an old man and accompanied by an amateur brass band.

It was in Jingshan Park that the first amateur chorus group was formed; today, the chorus groups there are of higher level. Even CCTV (China Central Television) produced a program on the activities, called *All People Singing on the Square of Passion*. On Sundays, there are usually more than 10 choirs of considerable size, including many small groups or pairs practicing by themselves in the park.

Professor Gao has been active in Jingshan Park chorus group for more than a decade, and many people in the park know her. This slender 80-year-old lady still has a melodious, sonorous voice, rare for her age. This Sunday, she went to a small chorus group of only 20 members, who greeted her and invited her to sing the song *China, I Love You!* Without a

1

Professor Gao and Master Ge

It was a Sunday morning. Retired physics professor Gao got up very early and prepared breakfast for her husband and herself. The breakfast was simple: a cup of milk, a piece of bread with jam. Afterwards she watered the flowers in the balcony. For Professor Gao, the two-day weekends were the most enjoyable of all her time. The previous morning, their son, who is studying physics at the Massachusetts Institute of Technology, phoned to chat with his parents as he did every

Saturday.

Around 10 o'clock this morning, Professor Gao finished her lunch and left home with a bag and a parasol. She got on a bus and soon arrived at Jingshan Park after several stops. Despite the scorching sun, there were many visitors from all parts of China in the park. Noticeably there were groups of people standing in the shade of ancient trees, practicing chorus singing. These groups were of 10 to several hundred. The largest one gathered close to the east gate. More

▶ An old man leads a group in practicing a song for the Beijing Olympic Games in a Beijing park.

throughout China. The songs include melodious folk ballads, new songs composed for the reform and opening up, and folk and pop songs created after China's opening up to the outside world, in addition to those from the former Soviet Union and the "cultural revolution".

These chorus groups are usually not organized by any organizations and are of various sizes and levels. Some large groups have several hundred members or even a thousand while smaller ones have 20-30 people or only around 10. Some large groups may have amateur bands, while smaller ones may only have a couple of accordions or even without any music accompanying. With or without music accompanying, the singers are always very enthusiastic and some perform quite professionally.

Apart from middle-aged and senior citizens in the amateur chorus, there are also some young people who have dreams and want to change their lives....

China has had rapid economic development over the last decade, why have amateur chorus groups become so popular among the people? Why do people choose singing? And what does chorus singing bring to the participants, mostly retirees or would-be retirees?

word, she started to sing the song to the accompany of an accordion.

> Birds flying in the blue sky,
> China, I love you!
> I love the jade-like sea in the south;
> I love the snow in the north.
> I love the boundless forests;
> I love the rolling mountains.
> I love the winding streams,
> which flow into my dreams.
> I will devote my youth,
> To China, my mother!

Some visitors were attracted by her singing and stopped to listen. Professor Gao loved this song because it brought her back to her youth.

At the age of 20, she left her hometown in Jiangsu Province and went to study in a college in Beijing as her parents had expected. At college, she joined the student chorus group because singing had

▼ Elderly amateur musicians accompanied the chorus singing.

been her hobby since elementary school. In the early 1950s when China was recovering from many years of war, the liberation had brought people pride and confidence to begin a new life. Many songs appeared during that period, eulogizing the nation, the life and the people.

China's ethnic minority areas also had remarkable changes as a result of state support for the cultural conservation and economic development of those areas. Many folk songs were discovered, revised or composed by musicians and were widely spread among the people; some even became household repertoires. The student chorus group Gao belonged to was extremely active in rehearsing and performing. After hours of studying physics and other subjects everyday, this added more color to her boring life.

Gao's interest in chorus singing makes her the most energetic in her family of three physicists. She benefited a lot from the weekly chorus singing in Jingshan Park not only morally but also physically. According to her, the vocal and pneumonic exercise in singing is good for improving lung capacity and facilitating metabolism. Moreover, the melodies and lyrics of the old songs would bring people back to their youth — psychologically beneficial for the aged.

For physics professor Gao, chorus singing is her hobby after retirement; but for disabled worker Ge, it is a moral support after he was injured in a traffic accident. After that, he joined the singing group at the Temple of Heaven.

Seven years ago, Ge had a traffic accident in which he was seriously injured with legs paralyzed and prospopospasm. Two cerebral operations left him two 10-cm-long scars and damaged half of his teeth. His arms were also partly paralyzed.

Ge was once a very talented mechanic in a factory, but the accident changed his entire life. It was extremely hard for him to know that he would spend the rest of his life in a wheelchair though his medical expenses were covered by insurance. He was only 45 and the financial income of the family mainly depended on him. He felt more pressure on him and became depressed and bad-tempered. The atmosphere at home grew more and more tense.

Ge's wife quit her job to look after her disabled husband. She was very much worried and felt helpless in comforting her depressed and irascible husband, until one day when she wheeled her husband into the Temple of Heaven near their home.

The Temple of Heaven, built in 1420 and covering 273 hectares, is the largest imperial park in China for worshipping the heaven in the old days. The buildings in the Temple were constructed in the harmony of the heaven, the earth and the gods, reflecting the ancient Chinese people's views on the universe and their architectural concepts. Now the Temple of Heaven was included in the World Heritage List by UNESCO in December 1998.

For tourists to Beijing, it is a place they must visit. For locals, it is a park for fun. The former imperial temple has now become a public park. Each morning, local residents come to the park to practice dancing, shadow boxing, gymnastics or *Qigong*, to play ball games or to take a walk around. Some other people sing old songs or recite opera pieces while music can be heard everywhere in the park. Foreign tourists are attracted to take snaps of the scenes that they won't see in other countries.

Six years ago, Ge and his wife entered this park, and had their course of life changed.

On that morning, when the couple went into the Imperial Music Court, they heard chorus singing, which guided them into a small woods where they saw many middle-aged and older people sitting in a circle singing old songs, with a man in his fifties as the conductor. The couple immediately joined in the singing since the songs were so familiar to them.

In the six years since that morning, the couple attended every session of singing. Singing has given them confidence

▶ The Hall of Prayer for Good Harvest, a magnificent building in the Temple of Heaven, is now considered as a landmark of Beijing.

Everyday, people practice *Taiji*, dancing or other exercises in the Temple of Heaven.

and a sense of belonging. Ge is well cared by other members of the group and his wheelchair is always placed at the center of the circle so that he can clearly see the gestures of the chorus conductor. Sitting in his wheelchair, Ge tries to follow the rhythm of the songs by clapping his inflexible hands and singing in a trembling voice. It is extremely hard for him, but singing gives him happiness and is good for health recovering. Six years of chorus singing helped improve his speaking ability, and he also found it the most delightful thing to do everyday.

Ge's wife is deeply impressed by the changes of her husband. "A sudden accident disabled a strong man and made him depressed," she said. "I took care of him but he often lost temper, and this sometimes made me annoyed. The members in the singing group all helped him, making him feel better and giving him advices for treatment and recovery."

"They are of the same age as Ge, and most of them are lay-offs or pensioners who also have financial difficulties. Chorus singing makes them forget these unhappy things. Ge had a quick recovery, beyond the expectation of his doctors."

Chorus singing brings hope as well as fun to ordinary workers like Ge.

2

New Values in Life

If you key in the name "Li Luzheng" at the search engines Baidu or Google, there may come out 6,030 and 4,220 web-pages respectively, all concerning him. There are also 266 posts about him on Baidu.

Who is Li Luzheng?

He is one of millions of rural labor-ers who have migrated to the cities. He is a farmer who became famous overnight by composing and singing his own songs.

"Actually, it's like a dream to sing on television," said him.

In the CCTV evening program of the Lantern Festival in February 2007, Li Luzheng, a laborer from Chengde, Hebei Province, sang a song named *Waving Hands*, which was composed by himself. The song tells about the lives of millions of rural laborers. Satural and sentimental, Li's song soon became popular among the farmer migrants. Li, himself, is an example

▼ In April 2007, Li Luzheng sang his song, *Waving Hands*, to the laborers at the "Bird's Nest" construction site.

of how rural workers can change their lives through hard work. He chose music for his success.

Li Luzheng came from a farmer family in a small mountain village in Longhua County, Chengde, about 300 kilometers north of Beijing. When he was young, his family was too poor to let him continue schooling, so he had to quit from junior middle school. He then wanted to work in a big city.

Believing that Beijing was the "heaven for laborers", he left home with a dozen yuan, and took a train with his former classmates to Beijing. His parents knew nothing about his whereabouts.

His first job was to work on a construction site in Liuliqiao of Fengtai District. Since he was too young and unskilled, he could only do some simple work like mixing lime and moving bricks. He only earned 6.5 yuan a day. However, he was happy about his job. He and his schoolmates chatted a lot about their dreams to wear leather shoes and walk around like city dwellers.

However, their dreams were smashed by an accident on a May evening. Their foreman asked Li and his fellow laborers to work overtime to dig sand, but Li went away because his elder sister had come to see him. Early the following morning, a truck driver came to tell him that two of his schoolmates were buried alive under the sand piles.

"Why did they die so young, after they left their parents only two months ago?" cried Li Luzheng. Even after many years whenever he mentioned his two friends, he still cannot help shedding tears.

Depressed, he went back home and helped his parents on the farm. He was shocked by the accident, and also learned that such tragedies happened very often. He later wrote this into his songs.

He went back to Beijing to work in 1997, 2000 and 2002, becoming more familiar with the city.

He and his fellow workers lived a poor life. Listening to the radio was their only entertainment everyday to pass monotonous time. There was only one radio, sometimes two, in a dormitory for over a hundred workers, and they often enjoyed pop songs from the radio.

Li Luzheng liked music very much. He first followed the songs broadcast on the radio, then gradually he felt unsatisfied with the songs written by others since there were no songs specially for rural workers. He had an impulse idea — why not compose his own songs?

One evening, Li Luzheng and his friends had a dinner party to welcome the father of one of his fellow workers who came to visit his son. The father tried to persuade his son to return home. This moving scene reminded Li of his own parents, and he suddenly had a desire to compose a song for the rural workers.

Li began his creation immediately. He first wrote what he thought and felt.

Since he had only received limited education and had no training in music, he tried but failed — the lyrics he wrote did not rhyme at all.

During the Dragon Boat Festival in 2006, he had a sick leave after he had injured his eye. Lying in bed, he missed his home and his aged parents. He then began to revise his lyrics by imitating the format of pop songs. A month later, he finished the song which he was rather satisfied with, because he thought the song perfectly expressed his feelings. His fellow workers helped him think of a proper title for the song, but their suggestions did not work. One day he saw a mother waving to her child from a crowded bus, and a title for the song came into his mind: *Waving Hands.*

Now Li Luzheng needed to write music for his song. He had no idea about music notes. However, he tried to create by himself according to the rhythm of the lyrics. He recorded his own singing on his mobile phone, but it sounded so different every time he sang the song. He realized that it might be necessary to find somebody to write down the music notes for him.

However, he could not find that kind of person since he did not have a proper job to make money. Until one day when he was singing his song loudly on a square, he was stopped by a middle-aged man who was playing a flute there.

"The song sounds quite melodious. Who composed it?" asked the man.

He was surprised to know that Li Lu-zheng had composed it himself. Li then asked him if he knew something about music notes, and whether he would write it down for him. The man agreed.

The two of them went to a small restaurant where they began their work. The man was called Li Benyou, a music teacher from Henan Province. He first played the flute according to Li Luzheng's singing, and had it recorded. He then invited Li

Luzheng to his place, and both finished the work in one week's time.

Li Luzheng began to practice his song. He sang for his fellow workers, who told him that the song truly expressed their feelings. He sang for local residents, who were moved to tears. He also sang for diners at roadside restaurants, who invited him to eat and drink with them.

He was proud of being able to tell others the emotions of rural workers through his song.

One day, a reporter from *Beijing Legal Evening* happened to hear his song and wrote a report "Rural Worker Created a Homesick Song Which Moves Local Residents." The report told a touching story about a rural farmer from Hebei who taught others to sing his song *Waving Hands*. The director of the CCTV Spring Festival Evening Show read the report and invited Li Luzheng, via the reporter, to participate in the preliminary screening. Li was very delighted.

On the afternoon of November 24, 2006, Li appeared at CCTV and sang his song in front of the directors. He was then asked to wait for the result.

He was so elated that even smiled in dreams, believing that his parents would be happy to watch his performance on television.

From that day on, he kept on practicing for fear that he might lose face if he did not sing well. His fellow workers also encouraged him. They were all eager to see his performance on TV.

About two weeks before the Spring Festival, Li was informed by the director that he had not been chosen for the New Year Eve Show. He and his co-workers were all very disappointed.

Unexpectedly, three days before the Lantern Festival, the director called Li again and asked him to participate in the rehearsal for the Lantern Festival Evening Show. At around 8:55 that evening, Li Luzheng appeared on the stage in a blue working suit and sang:

> When you are still enjoying the
>   festival,
> I'm already on the way to work.
> Saying goodbye to my family and
>   to my sweetheart,
> I recall the days we were together.
> Waving goodbye to my sweetheart,
> You know I'll miss you;
> Waving goodbye to my sweetheart,
> Please take care of our aged parents.
> I'll work very hard,
> For our happy life in the future.
>
> Train's whistle reminds me of depar-
>   ture,
> I had no choice but to leave.
> Waving goodbye to my sweetheart,
> When the buildings are completed,
> Snow falls and winter comes,
> When I'll be going back home.
> Waving goodbye to my sweetheart,
> You'll also be busy at home.

Waving goodbye to my sweetheart,
Please take care of our aged parents.
For a better life in the future,
We part for the time being.
The work is hard, but there'll be re-
    turn,
We'll surely have a better life.

His honest singing impressed the audience who applauded heartily. For him, it
was an incredible experience.

After the show, he rushed back to his
dormitory excitedly, with tears in eyes. He
was welcomed warmly by his fellow workers. "You were on TV!" they exclaimed.
The following day, his sister called and
told him that their parents had seen his
performance. Li said: "I haven't been
home for four years, and this year I went
home via TV."

Li Luzheng's story quickly spread on
the construction site. The workers began
to sense their hopes. Some followed Li to
sing, some began to play flute, and others

bought their musical in-
struments.

Almost overnight, Li Luzheng became a pop star for millions of rural workers. Many wanted to follow his footprints, while others gave him support and encouragement on the internet. One post read, "Although the plainly-dressed Li Luzheng appeared a little nervous on the stage, his performance really impressed the audience; no one cared about this little fault, because his voice was so sincere that it touched people's hearts."

Another post read,

▶ Li Luzheng is practicing guitar. He knows that he needs more practice before success.

"It is wonderful that Li Luzheng performed on television to sing for all the people in China. Millions of rural laborers have contributed so much to the development of our cities. They never expect any appreciation from the city dwellers. What they care about is to go back home after work and live a better life. This sincere hope moves the rural workers in China."

With unremitting efforts, Li Luzheng has changed his own life. Now his songs are sung by rural laborers all over the country. His experience has encouraged his fellow workers, as

▲ Li Luzheng singing for the workers and students at the National Aquatics Center construction site in April 2007.

Li said, "A new age for rural workers has come."

Li Luzheng had a new career of creating songs, while retired Mr. Han found new funs through music.

Mr. Han used to be a media editor and retired three years ago. One day, he went to Jingshan Park and saw people singing in chorus. The songs they sang were mostly old ones composed in the 1950s or 1980s, none reflecting the current times. He thought that there should be new songs for the new age, songs to reflect the country's reform and opening up. But there were very few like these, so he made up his mind to compose some.

What should be the theme of the songs? For him, it would not be difficult to write the lyrics to a song since he loved literature and music since childhood and had worked as a reporter and editor. However, it was no easy job to write a song which would be popular and came up with the time.

In 2005, China began the preparation for the Beijing Olympic Games. Mr. Han found that "one world, one dream" was just right for the theme of his first song.

"One world, one dream", the new Olympic slogan, embodied the idea of harmony, which was the core concept of the Games. It was also the ideal of the Chinese people to share the Chinese civilization and the future with the people of the rest of the world. Han then concentrated on the creation, revised and sometimes even started again, before he finally finished with a draft song.

On September 18, 2005, Han brought his song "One World, One Dream" to Jingshan Park, teaching people there to sing the song. It was an immediate success. Han was convinced that his songs for the new age would become popular.

After that, Han devoted all his time

to composing more songs, like *Smile Is My Namecard* and *Song of Laborers*. On the day the 2008 Olympic torch was lit, he composed the song *Light Enthusiasm to Disseminate the One Dream*. Later, the newspaper *The First* organized an activity to collect songs for the torch relay, and received hundreds of letters within a very short period. Many citizens wrote letters or called in to express their best wishes for the torch relay. Han submitted six of his songs to the newspaper office, and the song *Forward, Torch Bearers!* was awarded a prize.

Good music should match the rhythm of the lyrics. Han paid equal attention to both music and lyrics. Over the last three years, he created more than 100 songs. In addition to the songs closely related with big events in the country, he also composed music for poems, both ancient and modern, both Chinese and foreign. One such poem was Tang Emperor Li Yi's famous *ci*-poem *Yumeiren*:

With the passing of spring flowers and autumn moon,
How many old stories do I remember?

And Xu Zhimo's *Farewell to Cambridge:*
I leave gently, like gently I came;
I wave gently, saying goodbye, to the western sky.

He tried to achieve a harmony between music and words, especially for the two poems, which he revised for many times. Now the two poem songs have become the most popular ones in Jingshan Park.

"Why don't you sing old songs?"

"Why did you take so much effort to create and teach new songs?"

These questions are the ones frequently asked. Some foreign journalists also interviewed him.

Once a German reporter asked, "Do the older people who sing those old songs miss that time when the living standards were low and the society was relatively just? Are they dissatisfied with the present society so that they sing old songs and revolutionary songs?" Han said to the reporter, people would not engage in cultural, artistic or religious activities unless they have solved their basic living problems, as once said by a philosopher. These middle-aged people and pensioners come to the park to sing because they don't have to worry about their basic needs, and their living standards

▶ Mr. Han is teaching the group his song *Farewell to Cambridge*.

▲ Chorus singing brings these middle-aged and older people back to their youth.

have improved. This is the result of China's reform and opening-up.

People sing these old songs because they reminded them of their youth, he said. Moreover, the songs are pleasant to listen to and easy to sing. People treasure their present lives since their dreams have come true, as it is portrayed in the songs.

Old songs are classics, Han said, so that they are sung by people of all ages. However, he added, it is also necessary to create new songs to reflect the present time. So he composed *Beijing Welcomes You* to show his support for the Olympic Games; he created *The Song of China-Soviet Friendship* while Chinese leaders were visiting Russia. Immediately after the Wenchuan Earthquake on May 12, 2008, he wrote the song *To be Together with the People in Quake Area*. Seven days after the earthquake, he brought his new song to Jingshan Park and handed out over 100 copies of the song. A few days later, a singer contacted Han and told him that he

▲ Singing brings joy to these middle-aged and older people.

intended to sing the song at a quake-relief program.

Three years of experience of composing songs has given him a new life, and he also realized he could continue to work for the society after retirement. He has fun and new values in life, as described in his song *Singing in Jingshan*:

Here are many old stories
And historical changes.
Here is this unique garden in which

Thousands of people sing under
 ancient trees.
A scene that is not seen elsewhere,
Many people say.
Never seen so many people so happy
 here,
Many visitors say.
Never miss such a beautiful scene,
Many friends say.
Harmonious melody attracts people
 from everywhere.
Play your accordion,
I'll sing a new song,
To eulogize the new life.

3

Singing Edifies Both Singer and Audience

A media report said that, during evenings in Beijing, one may see *yangge* (a popular rural folk dance) teams dancing in the street and various activities in the parks like singing, drawing, playing chess and exercising.

The weekend chorus singing in Jingshan Park is one of the recreational activities. People from all parts of the city gather around a pavilion near the east gate of the park, singing Chinese and foreign songs. Among them are old couples, families of three generations, as well as boys and girls. Songs can even be heard outside the park.

In recent years, chorus singing has become one of the most popular cultural activities in Beijing. There are many singing competitions for people of different ages — the May Flower Singing Competition, Senior Chorus Competition, Beijing Chorus Festival, Beijing Student Chorus Festival, etc. In Jingshan Park, chorus singing, first started by ordinary citizens, has now become

▶ Jingshan Park of Beijing is famous for its peony flowers, which grow around the five pavilions on the hill in spring and summer.

a special part of the park and is widely known as the "Jingshan Phenomenon".

Jingshan is located to the north of the Forbidden City. It was originally an earthen hill formed by the earth dug up from the moat around the imperial palace. During the Qing Dynasty (1644-1911), Emperor Qianlong, a lover of poetry and nature, renamed it Jingshan (the Hill of Grand View) and included it as part of the imperial complex.

After the founding of the People's Republic of

▶ These middle-aged and older people who learned to play musical instruments when they were young, accompany the chorus.

China in 1949, the government renovated the original five pavilions, planted trees and grass, and turned it into a public park. On a fine day, one may have a panoramic view of Beijing from the Wanchun Pavilion at the top of the hill.

The first Jingshan chorus appeared in 1992. One rainy day in summer that year, a group of middle-aged and older people were resting in a pavilion on the hill. It started to rain heavily, so they had to wait there for the rain to stop. As they became impatient, a middle-aged man stood up and volunteered to sing songs for them.

He was named Hou, and was a music teacher. He sang some old popular songs in the 1950s, and was soon joined by others. From that day on, this small group gradually grew into the present-day Jingshan Ziguang Chorus Group, the first chorus group in Jingshan Park.

The Ziguang Chorus Group sings songs mainly in the 1950s and 1960s. On

▲ These middle-aged and older people play musical instruments in Jingshan Park every weekend.

each gathering, *The Ode to the Motherland* is always the second last song they sing, followed by *Unforgettable Evening* when all the members wave their hands for farewell. That is the most excited moment.

An accordion or a flute is usually played as accompaniment, and words are written on a big piece of paper, hanging on the pavilion pillar. People stand around the pavilion. Some groups have different vocal sections, for instance, male and female duets. Chorus conductors sometimes also teach the group singing skills, arousing the enthu-

▶ Enjoy dancing inside a pavilion.

siasm of the singers. They are often surrounded by big audiences who are deeply impressed by their sincerity and enthusiasm.

Anyone who likes singing can join in. So the singers are of different levels, affecting the overall effect of chorus. Therefore, some semi-experts volunteered to be chorus conductors. Some bring their own musical instruments. Everybody contributed to the chorus which becomes bigger each day.

Many other chorus groups appeared in other parks following the Jing-

▶ A woman dancing with the accompaniment of mouth organs.

Singing the song *Moscow Suburb Evening* (a folk song from the former Soviet Union) to the accompaniment of an accordion.

shan Park chorus group. The original chorus group in Jingshan Park has grown from one to a dozen groups, categorized into different types of songs, such as the songs of the former Soviet Union, bel canto songs, minority ethnic songs and foreign songs. Amateur dancers also volunteer to perform.

At present, there are chorus groups in almost all the parks in Beijing, including Beihai, the Temple of Heaven, Yuyuantan, Taoranting and Zizhuyuan. The participants are no longer local residents, and migrant workers and young people have also been members. When a large group sings popular songs such as *The Sun in the East* or *Ode to the Motherland*, everyone present at the scene, impressed by their energy and enthusiasm, also joins in.

The Voice of the Temple of Heaven Chorus Group, the first one in the park, used to have 600 to 700 members. Later some of its members left and formed small groups which can now be seen everywhere in the park. The present chorus conductor, Mr. Wang, used to be a salesman before retirement. He has been a music lover since school days, and is now a regular member of the chorus. Every morning, he conducts the chorus of over a hundred people for an hour, before singing with a lady pop songs for half an hour. The song is sung to accompany a dance called *Sixteen Steps*, which gives the group time to relax. The members of the chorus group enjoy moral cultivation as well as physical exercise.

Music can heal inner wounds and bring people together as friends. Music is the medicine for the heart and the cultivation of the mind. During the quick pace of China's economic development, singing can help people recover from psychosis.

4

Self-cultivation and Social Work

At the 14th Asian Culture and Art Festival, held in Columbus of Ohio in May 2008, a chorus group of 18 singers from China staged a spectacular performance. These amateur singers, all in their sixties, had heavenly voices, according to local media. It was the Love on the Grassland Chorus Group, formed by people from Beijing who used to work on the grass-lands of Inner Mongolia in the 1960s and 1970s. Their love for the society and their contribution to the society, well known in Beijing, are fully displayed in their songs.

Founded on July 9, 1999, the group

mainly consists of Beijing residents who used to work in the Xilin Guole League, Inner Mongolia.

"Educated youth" was a very special term used in modern China. In China, "educated youths" refer to those urban youths who went to the countryside

to work as farmers in the 1950s to 1970s either voluntarily or forced to. Most of them did not finish their junior or senior secondary education. The total number ranged between 12 to 18 million.

In the 1960s and 1970s when the government launched the campaign

▶ Members of the Love on the Grassland Chorus Group visiting the United States.

of "going to work in the countryside or mountainous areas", more than 100,000 "educated youths" from all over China went to Inner Mongolia. Among them were 4,000 Beijingers, who settled down in the Xilin Guole League of Inner Mongolia.

Ms. Ma Xiaoli, the initiator and leader of the chorus group, went to Inner Mongolia when she was 20. The local people on the grassland well received this young girl, despite that her family was labeled with "political problems". Ma Xiaoli was very grateful to the people on the grassland who were like her mother.

"They were so kind and sincere," she said. "When I was to leave the grassland, I did not tell anyone but left quietly. I climbed slopes and walked for more than an hour, and then turned my head to see the villagers still waving goodbye to me."

"The scene is still lingering in my mind. I will never forget it."

For Ma Xiaoli and her fellow youths,

their years on the grassland had left indelible impressions on them. Most of them have returned to Beijing, but emotionally they still belong to the grassland. According to Ma Xiaoli, "My feeling for my second hometown is stronger than that for my native place, because I spent my youth — the most beautiful and purest period of time — there. Life there was tough, but I was edified by the Mongolian culture which had changed me completely."

Many former "educated youths" now want to do something good for their "second hometown". In 1999, Ma and her former friends set up the Love on the Grassland Chorus Group.

As one of the major singers in the group, Hai Yin regards the group as a gift for her.

In 1969, Hai Yin, 16 year old, left her home in Zhejiang Province, a water town south of the Yangtze River, traveled all the way to the dry grasslands of Inner Mongolia. She spent her youth there and left when she was 30. That was an important period of her growth from an innocent girl to a mature adult. During her 14 years there, Hai Yin worked as an actress and creator in an art troupe. Today she is over 50 but she is reliving her youth in the chorus group.

In May 2008, while the chorus group was in Columbus, a great earthquake shocked Wenchuan of Sichuan. The group immediately decided to donate all the income from their performance to the quake-hit areas. At the same time, they composed songs to help rise the enthusiasm in the quake relief. Hai Yin joined in the chorus and recited a poem written specially for the relief. Today, she serves as the head of the dance team of the group. She sees that the group has a higher realm that cultivates mind, and she appreciates every opportunity the group offers her.

Owing to the strong affection for their "second hometown", Hai Yin and other members of the group paid several visits to the grasslands in recent years. Through these visits, they learned more about the place and the people there. The Mongolian people do not like to talk much, but they have the character of nature — open-minded, brave and tolerant — coming along with their living environment. This is reflected in their daily life. The sincerity and kindness of the people on the grassland carved deep in Hai Yin's mind.

The members of the chorus group are all amateur singers, and 90 percent of them have never performed on stage. How could they overcome all the difficulties and continue singing to this day? "Because we had spent our young lives on the grassland, and our love for the grassland and its people will never fade," said Hai Yin.

All the former "educated youths" who had lived on the grassland share the same affection. Today, some of them are still living on the grassland, some have returned to cities, and others have gone abroad. Some are successful in career, and others are laid off. However, their sincere love for the grassland has not been changed, and they always want to help the people when they come across difficulties.

On January 4, 2001, two former "educated youths" learned from their friends on the grassland that an unexpected snowstorm had struck the whole Inner Mongolia for 70 hours, and the temperature there was down to minus 50 degrees Centigrade. Soon this news arrived at the group, and all the members wanted to do something for the Xilin Guole League.

Almost immediately, the former "educated youths" in Beijing gathered to discuss ways to help the people on the grassland. Someone suggested a charity performance to raise money, but according to regulation it could not accept public donations because it was not a professional group. Ma Xiaoli, the head of the group, then sought help from the

China Charity Association, which decided to help the Love on the Grassland Chorus Group hold a charity performance. The same afternoon, the group members and staff from the Charity Association bought with their own money 2,000 cases of instant noodles and two truckloads of leather coats for the Xilin Guole League. This was the first batch of relief material to arrive at the grassland, even before the snowstorm was reported by the media.

According to Ma, on January 13, the chorus group started rehearsal for the performance, and some tried to locate the venue or arrange the sale of tickets. The former "educated youths" also made some landscape pictures and artworks for charity sale. Preparations for the performance went on quite smoothly.

On the evening of January 20, 2001, the first charity show was held at the Hall of the Minzu Palace, and the second one at the auditorium of the China Academy of Social Sciences. Both were very successful. The audience was deeply impressed by the old Mongolian songs that they were very familiar with, and the on-site donations totaled 900,000 yuan. Donations from abroad amounted to four million yuan. This showed that the chorus group and the people on the grassland

▼ The Love on the Grassland Chorus Group often participates in charity shows, winning acclaim from the society.

were closely related to each other. Since then, public welfare has become a major work of the group in addition to rehearsal and performance.

Mongolian music is an expression of the mind, bringing people serenity and bliss. It usually creates a consonance between the singers and audience. For the members of the group, singing not only keeps the memories of their youth, but also purifies their minds. It also serves as a communication channel between the cities and the grassland.

Today, the chorus group is in its ninth year. Its membership has grown from 20 to over 100. On Sunday afternoons, the members meet at Ma Xiaoli's office for vocal exercises, while sipping milk tea. They all work hard to express their love for the grassland through their performance.

The group also has professional tutors, so its level has improved very fast. The group mainly sings songs from the grassland, and holds charity performances for environmental protection. It sets this as its mission and has won appreciation and support from former "educated youths", Mongolians and all those who love the grassland. The group is regarded as "our moral home" by the former "educated youths". The chorus group is now a member of the China World Culture Exchange Promotion Association, China Chorus Association and China Chorus League. It was invited by the associations to perform at various important art events including the ones held at the Beijing Music Hall and Beijing Zhongshan Park

▲ The Love on the Grassland Chorus Group
visiting the United States.

Music Hall.

The chorus group's professional skill has been widely recognized. In October 2001, the group was invited to perform at the Jiangmen International Chorus Festival, held in Jiangmen, Guangdong Province. At the Third International Olympic Chorus Festival held in Bremen in July of 2004, the group won the silver prize for folk chorus and another one for male chorus.

The members of the group remain modest after winning so many awards and so much praises. They have their mission in mind,

◀ Members of the Love on the Grassland Chorus Group express their love through their voices.

according to Ma Xiaoli, for the protection of the grassland and for the reservation of its beautiful scenery.

Their favorite song, *The Love on the Grassland,* best expresses their sentiments:

> Oh, grassland, my sweet home,
> Oh, horseback, my cradle of life.
> You fed me with your holy milk,
> And sang affectionate songs when I slept.
> The campfire, like sunglow, made me warm,
> The snow-white wool kept me from cold.
> Wherever I go, I hear the music of the horse-head violin,
> However far I go, I smell the flavor of milk tea.

5

Singing and Harmonious Society

Why do so many middle-aged and older people like to participate in chorus in parks? How do young people think about this?

As a DW reporter said, "It's quite a scene where hundreds of people gather to sing *The Sun in the East* in the park. What does this activity mean?"

They interviewed Professor Heberer of the Duisburg-Essen University, an expert on China's social science. He observed that people participating in the chorus were very happy; they sang revolutionary songs, and no one opposed the government or the Communist Party. However, not everyone comes for the same reason. Some people are idle, and others regard singing as a kind of physical exercise, especially those who are not so healthy. There are also some who are not so happy about the society.

If they're not allowed to sing, what will they do? They will feel more lonely or even resentful. If they could express their dissatisfaction through singing, it helps them feel at ease. So the government does not interfere but, instead, encourages such activities

▶ A man kicking shuttlecock.

which create a cultural atmosphere and maintain social harmony.

In fact, however, the reasons for middle-aged and older people to partici-

pate in chorus singing are much simpler than what the media or scholars of social science think. Some just want to kill time, and others like to develop hobbies. Still

Some people dancing with long ribbons of silk.

▲ Playing poker is popular among pensioners.

▲ A man singing Peking Opera.

others want to ease of their past unhappy experiences.

A Beijing reporter interviewed an old couple, who said that it was fun to sing and they enjoyed singing both old and new songs. They have made many new friends. Chorus singing has been their joy of life.

A middle-aged lady said that she goes to Yuyuantan Park on weekend mornings for physical exercise and chorus singing. She used to sleep a lot at home but always felt tired. Now singing has brought her energy and happiness.

◀ Playing music for self-entertainment.

▲ Chinese chess is a game loved by people of all ages.

As the reporter commented, one cannot really understand why people like these activities so much until one actually becomes one of them. Chorus singing satisfies the needs of middle-aged and older people for culture, and is also good for their health and family life.

Nowadays, chorus singing can be seen not only in Beijing but also in many other cities like Shanghai and Guangzhou.

Jingshan Park was the original place where chorus singing started, and now there is a Jingshan Chorus

▶ A 5-year-old boy plays mouth organ with his grandfather. Music gives him big fun.

▲ A lady in her seventies plays saxophone in a park and attracts a big audience.

Festival each year. Each summer, amateur chorus groups participate in the competition. After two rounds of competition, 12 groups enter the final in October, when it is the golden season of the year. Audience and media gather in the park to watch the final competition, one of the big events in Beijing.

Residential areas, companies, army, institutions, schools and even villages in Shanghai all organize chorus singings. They can be seen in 95 percent of the 120 parks in the city. The total number of chorus groups reaches 3,000, with millions of participants coming from all walks of life.

In Jiaxing of Zhejiang Province, chorus singing has become an everyday activity. According to the Jiaxing media, the enthusiasm for chorus singing has turned it into a popular cultural activity and a daily entertainment. The 10-year-old Jiaxing Xiucheng Chorus Group has won several awards since 1995, including

There is a mouth organ band in Beijing consisting of older people and directed by a silver-haired old man. When they play in the park, others join in to share the excitement.

▲ An amateur mouth orgn conductor

the third prize in a national chorus competition, and the first prize in the First Zhejiang Chorus Competition. The group also staged at the Nevers International Chorus Festival, France. Xu Yaxiang, a retired worker, recalls her experience at the festival, "Despite language barriers, we, together with Russian singers, sang Russian song *Katyusha*. It was an unforgettable thing in my life."

Chorus needs harmony among various vocal sections, and this requires all the participants to cooperate. So cooperation between people overcomes people's loneliness and stress. Many single men and women even found their partners through chorus activities.

For audience, chorus is a kind of entertainment and mind cultivation. "Chorus art is a common language that links the people in the world. Whenever and wherever there is chorus, the minds of the singers and audience will be connected," said Ron Salzmann, the chairperson of the International Chorus Association.

Young people usually support and understand their parents' chorus activities. You may see countless posts on the internet regarding chorus singing:

"I'm from Beijing and I have seen chorus in parks. It's great. They sing revolutionary songs as well as other old popular ones. There are also aged dancers. I think people from all over the world should go and see it because they are the most energetic people of their age."

"Whenever I listen to the chorus singing in Luxun Park in Shanghai, I always feel excited. I like such activities and I like to listen to their songs and share their enthusiasm."

"These singers grew up during the period of hardship yet sincerity and vigor, so their experience has integrated themselves with the songs of that time. They have never lost their passion, and that is a blessing for them."

"There are many people singing

songs in Litchi Park of Shenzhen. I sing with them. At the southeastern corner of the park is the huge portrait of Deng Xiaoping."

"There have been chorus groups in the Baiyun Hill in the northern part of Guangzhou for almost 10 years. On most mornings, the older people climb up to the top, sit down and sing revolutionary songs, one after another. The content of the songs reflect their true feelings. Songs of revolution, expressing people's sincere emotions, can last for a long time."

Today, China has entered a period of diversified lifestyles. People pursue different ways of living and the society also tolerate various lifestyles. Since 2007, Minsheng Life Insurance Co, Ltd. in Beijing has sponsored public art groups in 10 provinces and municipalities, including Beijing, Shanghai and Henan, where it has branches. According to the person in charge of the Project Sponsoring Public Chorus Activities in a Harmonious Society, Minsheng

Life Insurance has so far provided special funds to sponsor public chorus groups that abide by the laws and rules of the state. The company provides stereo equipment, musical instruments, venues for rehearsal, and transportation. Exchanges and professional training programs are also arranged to help improve the singers' levels.

In Beijing there are four groups that are sponsored by the company: Voice of Friendship Chorus Group, Haiyue Chorus Group, Yuye Chorus Group and Hongling Dancing Group.

Xu Peidong, a famous musician and member of the CPPCC, wrote an article describing the public chorus activities in Fuzhou. "When I arrived in Fuzhou, I learned that there were evening chorus groups in the parks, so I went to a park to have a look," he said. "I was fascinated by the singing of a chorus group called Happiness. They were singing songs of the Long March. The winter that year (2007)

▲ The Haiyue Chorus Group, sponsored by Min-sheng Life Insurance Co., Ltd., has a conductor and a band. It is the largest chorus group in Jingshan Park.

was colder than usual, but there were so many singers and audiences."

"At the other end of the square, a group called Voice on Lakeside was singing in Fuzhou dialect. Their enthusiasm for chorus was really beyond my expectation."

"I was very surprised at their chorus levels," he added. "Those amateur groups have reached professional level. You can clearly hear the different vocal sections in their singing. All this was the result of the local government's support for public cultural activities."

Xu said that music is a popular art and can help create a friendly atmosphere among people and a harmonious society.

It has long been part of the Chinese tradition to express one's feelings through poems and songs. While China is advancing rapidly in economy, people need culture and music — chorus singing in particular — which seems more relevant and significant.

图书在版编目（CIP）数据

来自百姓的歌声：英文 / 王洋，桔子著；石巍译.
北京：新世界出版社，2008.11
(国情故事)
ISBN 978-7-80228-998-7

I. 来　II.①王　②桔　③石　III.社会生活－概况－
中国－英文 IV.D669

中国版本图书馆CIP数据核字（2008）第177008号

Chorus Singing from the People
来自百姓的歌声

作　　者：王洋　桔子
策　　划：张海鸥
翻　　译：石巍（同文世纪）
图片提供：秦兆农　秦凤京　黑克　草原恋合唱团
责任编辑：李淑娟
封面设计：韩　英
责任印制：李一鸣　黄厚清
出版发行：新世界出版社
社　　址：北京市西城区百万庄大街24号（100037）
总编室电话：＋86 10 6899 5424　　68326679（传真）
发行部电话：＋86 10 6899 5968　　68998705（传真）
本社中文网址：http://www.nwp.cn
本社英文网址：http://www.newworld-press.com
版权部电子信箱：frank@nwp.com.cn
版权部电话：＋86 10 6899 6306
印　　刷：北京外文印刷厂
经　　销：新华书店
开　　本：787 × 1092　1/32
字数：30千字　　印张：3.375
版次：2009年1月第1版　2009年1月北京第1次印刷
书号：ISBN 978-7-80228-998-7
定价：19.80元